Making Dialogue Effective

The Dialogue Society is a registered charity, established in London in 1999, with the aim of advancing social cohesion by connecting communities through dialogue. It operates nation-wide with regional branches across the UK. Through localised community projects, discussion forums, teaching programmes and capacity building publications it enables people to venture across boundaries of religion, culture and social class. It provides a platform where people can meet to share narratives and perspectives, discover the values they have in common and be at ease with their differences.

Making Dialogue Effective

www.DialogueSociety.org
info@dialoguesociety.org
Tel: +44 (0)20 7619 0361

Dialogue Society
402 Holloway Road
London N7 6PZ

**DIALOGUE
SOCIETY**
LONDON 1999

First published in Great Britain 2013

© Dialogue Society 2013

Registered Charity No: 1117039

ISBN 978-0-9569304-6-0

Contents

Acknowledgements

The Dialogue Society extends heartfelt thanks to the speakers at our London 'Making Dialogue Effective' panel discussion series, some of whose insights are recorded in these pages:

Dr Jill Adam, Level Partnerships
Danny Chivers, Environmental Author and Activist
Lisa Cumming, Programme for a Peaceful City, University of Bradford
Dr Marwan Darweish, Centre for Peace and Reconciliation Studies, Coventry University
Dr Diana Francis, Conflict Transformation Facilitator, Trainer and Consultant
Justine Huxley, St Ethelburga's Centre for Reconciliation and Peace
Ozcan Keles, Dialogue Society
Dr Ute Kelly, Department of Peace Studies, University of Bradford
Simon Keyes, St Ethelburga's Centre for Reconciliation and Peace
Samuel Klein, Coexistence Trust[1]
Prof Ian Linden, Tony Blair Faith Foundation
Dr Nicola Montagna, Department of Criminology and Sociology, Middlesex University
Mehri Niknam MA, MBE, Joseph Interfaith Foundation
Sarah Perceval, Storyteller (specialising in sacred stories)
Canon David Porter, Director for Reconciliation at Coventry Cathedral
Imam Dr Abduljalil Sajid, Brighton Islamic Mission and Muslim Council for Religious and Racial Harmony UK
Alison Seabrooke, Community Development Foundation
Stephen Shashoua, Three Faiths Forum
Dr Andrew Smith, Scripture Union: Youth Encounter

Frances Sleap, Project Coordinator and Research Fellow at the Dialogue Society, has selected key insights from the discussions and presented them in the short articles contained in this volume.

Members of the Dialogue Society team have added their recommendations to those taken from the contributions of our speakers.

---

1   At the time of publication Samuel Klein has moved on from his post with the Coexistence Trust.

Foreword

This booklet is the product of several stages of a dialogical process. It began with an 'internal' dialogue at the Dialogue Society, in conversations between the directors and certain friends and advisers. Some of our friends are sceptical friends, who do us the service of asking difficult questions. Is dialogue not too theological and theoretical, too far removed from everyday realities to be socially relevant? Does it really extend beyond the tea-fuelled self-congratulation of a few liberal religious believers? The core of many of the questions we were facing was this: does dialogue have any *real* social effects, and could any such effects be augmented?

In response to these questions we opened up this dialogue on dialogue to a wider circle, inviting others professionally engaged in relevant projects to be part of a series of panel discussions scrutinising the aims, methods and achievements of dialogue. Through this extended dialogue we hoped to critically examine our own work and identify ways in which it could be improved.

We were delighted that so many experienced and insightful people responded to our request, and extend our heartfelt thanks to all our speakers, and to the other attendees who came, listened and gave their own thoughtful perspectives. We learnt a great deal in pondering with them the various difficulties in doing dialogue well[2] and in hearing of the various approaches and techniques which they had found fruitful in diverse contexts.

A selection of their insights and suggestions are presented in this booklet, along with a list of specific practical recommendations drawn from the discussions and from the Dialogue Society's own experience. We hope that others will benefit from the wealth of insights presented here and that this booklet will contribute to a valuable ongoing dialogue on dialogue.

I invite readers to keep the dialogue going by sending me any comments, ideas or suggestions. Alternatively you may wish to comment on the individual reports on the discussions in the 'columns' section of our website (http://www.dialoguesociety. org/columns.html).

Ozcan Keles
Executive Director

Dialogue Society
London, January 2013

---

2   I say 'well' because, as you will quickly notice in reading this volume, whether dialogue can or should be done 'effectively' is something of a contentious point!

Preface

The short chapters contained in this volume present some of the key insights offered by contributors to the Dialogue Society's 'Making Dialogue Effective' panel discussion series in London, which took place between November 2010 and March 2011. The six discussions brought together dialogue professionals, religious leaders, conflict resolution specialists, academics and other professionals with a wealth of relevant experience.

These professionals, and interested attendees from a range of professional and cultural backgrounds, together applied themselves to some of the challenges which often confront people working in dialogue with regard to its effectiveness. We are asked, or ask ourselves:

- Does what we do make a tangible difference to society in any way?
- Does our work, whether directly or otherwise, reach beyond the sympathetic to those whose attitudes and behaviour are an actual threat to peace and social cohesion?
- Are the relationships that our work initiates across cultural or religious boundaries of a meaningful and lasting kind?
- Is our work part of something broader that is capable of effecting change on a grand scale?

The series was intended to occasion focused and constructive discussion of such questions among a range of people concerned with relationships between different cultural, religious or social groups, in their professional lives or in a voluntary or personal capacity. We picked out six specific questions and invited speakers whose experience and expertise would provide valuable perspectives on that particular topic.

Many of our speakers, like the Dialogue Society, were professionally engaged in dialogue, intended to create or strengthen relationships between people of different faiths, world views, cultures, backgrounds and even professions in the UK and Ireland. Their techniques and experiences were diverse, allowing a helpful sharing of good ideas for community dialogue, as well as fruitful joint reflection on common challenges and pitfalls.

They also engaged in in-depth exploration of the goals and values of dialogue. In our first discussion, speakers quickly questioned the terms in which the discussion was framed, introducing discussion of what 'dialogue' is and of whether it is appropriate to talk of 'effectiveness' in this context. We identified a common sense, shared by the Dialogue Society, that dialogue is of great value in itself, apart from any social effects. Concern for dialogue to 'work' must be balanced with respect for the integrity of a mysterious and delicate process.

The perspectives of dialogue professionals were complemented by guests with experience of working with cultural diversity respectively in education and in community development and engagement: Jill Adam and Alison Seabrooke. Dr Nicola Montagna and Danny Chivers brought insights from another sphere. Their understanding and experience of social movements informed discussion of whether dialogue is, could, or should be a social movement, and what it might learn from other movements.

Conflict transformation experts, Dr Marwan Darweish and Dr Diana Francis, introduced us to the factors that can make or break a dialogue process in conflict situations. Their reflections gave those involved in dialogue in less fraught contexts a good deal of food for thought on the details that can help or hinder dialogue.

The overall aims of the series were as follows:

- To encourage inter-professional dialogue, interaction and cooperation between people working on intercultural/interreligious dialogue, peace and social cohesion.
- To foster dialogue between people engaged with dialogue at the personal or community level, and those concerned with the same questions in a professional capacity.
- To explore and clarify the questions of what effectiveness in dialogue is, and whether and how it can be measured.
- To find a range of creative and practical answers to the question of how dialogue can be made effective by
    - identifying and promoting current best practice and
    - identifying and promoting promising future possibilities.
- To share these answers among all participants of the series and more widely.

This short volume aims to fulfil the final aim listed above. It comprises a reflective article on each of the panel discussions, presenting key insights and suggestions. These articles were initially published in the columns section of the Dialogue

Society website, where they can still be accessed and commented upon (http://www.dialoguesociety.org/columns.html). In some cases, due to the complexity of the material, two columns were needed to do justice to the discussions; in these cases the articles here are presented in more or less the same form, in two parts. In addition to these articles we have included a list of specific recommendations drawn from the discussions and from the Dialogue Society's own experience.

Effectiveness in Intercultural and Interfaith Dialogue: Can It Be Defined? How Do We Measure It?

Part I

The first discussion of the 'Making Dialogue Effective' series brought together Dr Ute Kelly of the University of Bradford, Mehri Niknam MA, MBE of the Joseph Interfaith Foundation, Simon Keyes of St Ethelburga's Centre for Reconciliation and Peace and Dr Andrew Smith of the Scripture Union's Youth Encounter project. The discussion explored some contentious questions. Our panellists examined how useful managerial language of 'effectiveness' and 'measuring' was in the context of interfaith/intercultural dialogue. To comprehend this crucial issue we must first clarify what this dialogue *is*.

Participants brought different definitions to the table. They fall into two groups. The first covers formal definitions of dialogue, those truest to its etymological meaning of 'finding meaning through words' (Simon Keyes). David Bohm, William Isaacs and Martin Buber were cited as important thinkers about the philosophical nature of dialogue.[3] Daniel Yankelovich was also discussed.[4] Yankelovich characterises dialogue as speaking and listening under three conditions: equality, or at least suspension, as far as humanly possible, of inequality and coercive influences; listening with empathy in order to understand, and bringing assumptions out into the open (Ute Kelly). *Interfaith/intercultural* dialogue in these terms is such dialogue among participants of different faiths/cultures.

Andrew Smith noted that by so precise a definition Youth Encounter project may not have done any dialogue in the last ten years! Certainly various Dialogue Society projects fall outside such a definition. Both are interfaith/intercultural dialogue on an expanded definition along these lines: 'a range of activities through which people of different social, cultural and religious groups come together for meaningful interaction and exchange.' Considering the relation

---

3 See Martin Buber, *I and Thou*, (Simon and Schuster, 1971), *Between Man and Man* (Routledge, 2002); David Bohm, *On Dialogue*, (Routledge, 2004); William Isaacs, *Dialogue and the Art of Thinking Together* (Bantam Doubleday Dell, 1999).

4 See Daniel Yankelovich, *The Magic of Dialogue*, (Simon and Schuster, 1999).

between the two definitions we could perhaps say this: dialogue in the formal sense takes the meaningful interaction aspired to by dialogue in the broad sense and explores its capacities to the full under, relatively speaking, 'ideal' conditions.

We can now turn to the issue of the appropriateness of the term 'effectiveness'. Ute Kelly suggested that 'effective dialogue' might even be a paradox. Effectiveness means 'power to bring about a desired or expected result.' But seeing dialogue in these instrumental terms, desiring or expecting it to bring about particular results, can reduce the chances of genuine dialogue occurring. Dialogue can have a range of valuable results. Apart from the deeper understanding of self and others which inevitably results from good dialogue it may bring trust, build relationships and give the possibility of personal change. Ute Kelly and Simon Keyes both suggested that prescribing specific outcomes for dialogue, whether these results or others, risks undermining the essential exploratory characteristic of the dialogic interaction and interfering with the natural dynamic flow of connection between participants. This could apply as well to dialogue in the broader sense as to dialogue in the formal sense. Positive human effects and social goods are perhaps more likely to issue from the dialogue if it is allowed to be free and unpredictable, and not required to be 'effective' according to notions of effectiveness taken from other contexts.

These reservations about the 'managerial' language of effectiveness gives pause for thought, because of course organisers of dialogue often have desired effects in mind beyond the process of dialogue itself. The Dialogue Society, for example, aims to advance the goal of social cohesion. Even pioneers of dialogue in the formal sense sometimes have visions of far-reaching effects. 'Dialogue: a Proposal', which outlines Bohmian dialogue begins with this statement: *'Dialogue... is a way of exploring the roots of the many crises that face humanity today.'* [5]

But Bohmian dialogue hopes to address crises not by analysing the crises themselves, but by allowing dialogue to give participants new insight into the thought processes which contribute to them. The dialogue is allowed to take its own course, without restrictions on subject areas or direction. It is given space to develop organically.

This is one of the key insights from our first panel discussion. Real dialogue requires space. We mustn't crowd it by being too prescriptive about what it must achieve. We may have concrete aspirations in mind and trust that dialogue will serve these, but we must allow it to do so in its own time, in sometimes unpredictable ways. Perhaps in doing so we will gain a heightened awareness of the intrinsic value of this creative human process of sharing and reflection.

---

5   David Bohm, Donald Factor and Peter Garrett, *Dialogue- A Proposal,* 1991. http://www. david-bohm.net/dialogue/dialogue_proposal.html

Effectiveness in Intercultural and Interfaith Dialogue: Can It Be Defined? How Do We Measure It?

Part 2

Part 1 of this article looked at a key issue raised by the questions of the first panel discussion: 'Can effectiveness in interfaith/intercultural dialogue be defined?' and 'How do we measure it?' That key issue was the appropriateness of the language of 'effectiveness' in this context. Panellists were concerned that thinking in such terms could actually prevent genuine dialogue occurring by putting participants under the pressure of external objectives. A key insight of the discussion was that real dialogue requires space. Crowding it with external objectives can be counterproductive.

Here we will use these insights to give answers to the initial questions of the panel discussion. We will also draw on further insights of the panel and participants for practical advice related to those answers.

Let us begin with the first question: Can effectiveness in interfaith/intercultural dialogue be defined? It is, we might say, problematic to define effectiveness in dialogue, because it is arguably ill-conceived to seek prescribed 'effects' from it. The real issue for dialogue practitioners is the *genuineness* of their dialogue. On Yankelovich's 'formal' definition, genuine dialogue would be defined as dialogue in which participants are able to suspend inequality and coercive influences, to listen with empathy, seeking understanding, and to bring assumptions into the open. On the broader definition of dialogue genuine dialogue would involve, a little less ambitiously, meaningful interaction and exchange between participants, in which participants are able to speak to each other with some honesty and listen to each other attentively. The closer participants in dialogue in the broad sense are able to come to the ideal of Yankelovich's three conditions, we might argue, the more meaningful their interaction and exchange will be. It is from *genuine* dialogue, in the experience of panellists and participants, that transformative personal and interpersonal results are most likely to issue. These in turn may ultimately lead to positive social effects.

Panellists offered various reflections on how genuine dialogue can be promoted. A conscious effort might be made to leave space for creative human things to happen in dialogue by consciously avoiding instrumentalisation. Dialogue facilitators might try constantly checking the presence of Yankelovich's conditions and looking to restore them when they are found to be absent. On a personal level, participants may make conscious efforts to be fully present in the dialogue, avoiding distractions and attending to genuine, empathic listening (Ute Kelly).

Simon Keyes noted the importance of safety in creating the conditions for dialogue. Danger is not limited to physical danger, and where people feel in any kind of danger they will not feel free to engage in dialogue.

As Mehri Niknam noted, for dialogue practitioners, methods allowing genuine dialogue are generally learnt through experience, through trial and error. Building up the conditions for meaningful interaction to take place demands time and persistence. It often takes potential participants quite some time to develop sufficient trust in the facilitator to be ready to engage.

To turn to our second question, can we measure the effectiveness, or the genuineness of dialogue? Dr Kelly noted that the genuineness of dialogue, and its immediate effects in terms of understanding and personal transformation are best captured qualitatively (as opposed to quantitatively), through dialogic examinations, and reflective, dialogue-based writing. Perhaps some of the columns beginning to accumulate on the Dialogue Society website will be able to encapsulate some of the character and effects of dialogue.

What might be measured quantitatively is the question of who is being exposed to the potentially transformative effects of dialogue. Significantly for organisations such as the Dialogue Society, dialogue can only potentially contribute to any ultimate aspirations of harmonious interfaith/intercultural relations if sufficient people from different faith and/or cultural groups are exposed to it. If the 'vertical' reach of dialogue- the power of the effect it has on individuals, can only be measured qualitatively, its 'horizontal' reach- the numbers of individuals exposed in particular groups, can be carefully numerically analysed. Dr Smith noted that the charity he has recently founded ('The Feast') is embarking on major statistical analysis of who is coming, and who is coming back.

We will find, examining the other panel discussions in this series, that exposing diverse people to dialogue is an ongoing concern of many dialogue practitioners. Practitioners try a range of approaches to widen the appeal of dialogue. This is where dialogue according to the 'broader' definition can come into its own. People uninterested in intercultural dialogue per se may be interested in mountain biking with other young people of different faiths, or in engaging in social action with a culturally mixed group. Such activities can, sometimes, be the starting point of ultimately meaningful dialogue for broader audiences. Dialogue practitioners may find themselves balancing two concerns: making sure that people come to engage in dialogue, and making sure that what they engage in is a genuine dialogue.

Discussion 2

Effectiveness in Dialogue at the Grassroots: Seeking the Personal and the Genuine

The second panel discussion of our 'Making Dialogue Effective' series focused on how dialogue can reach beyond the superficial level of 'meeting and greeting'. How can we make dialogue a genuine interpersonal encounter which deepens mutual understanding and has the potential to transform relationships? Our panel consisted of Imam Dr Abduljalil Sajid, Storyteller Sarah Perceval and Samuel Klein, Co-Director of the Coexistence Trust.

A lot of the discussion was, in one way or another, about being creative, and about being brave. Creativity and courage, in a range of contexts, can break down the barriers to real interpersonal encounters.

Stories shared by our panellists demonstrated the impact that the courage and initiative of one or two individuals can have on the quality of relationships within their local community. Sarah Perceval told how she and a friend had a vision of living on a street where people knew each other, trusted each other and did not meet only in the event of a plumbing problem. They went out, somewhat nervously, to knock on the door of every house in the street. When they introduced themselves by saying 'Hello, we're your neighbours', they were generally warmly received. Now people meet for neighbours' brunches, and are invited to more spiritually based gatherings which provide a refuge of prayer and peace.

Imam Sajid and his wife, new to London in the 1970's, faced constant racist and Islamophobic abuse. When they moved to Brighton, they decided to take a proactive approach to their new community. They wrote to all their neighbours, introducing themselves and inviting them to tea. Within three months they had met and befriended everybody. Now their grandchildren are friends with their neighbours' grandchildren.

Such personal initiatives, perhaps, have something of a head start in the search for genuine dialogue. When an individual plucks up the courage to approach a neighbour, not knowing what their reaction will be, the encounter naturally begins in a personal, intimate space. The individual who opens herself up and puts herself in a vulnerable position invites an open, genuine response.

When we engage in dialogue in an organisational setting, more reflection is sometimes required to ensure that genuine dialogue can take place. Samuel Klein noted that formal habits associated with organisations can sometimes subtly distance us from one another. Sometimes choosing more casual clothing or deciding not to sit behind tables can remove a psychological barrier to personal encounters. We need to be self-aware, considering the messages that we send before even opening our mouths and considering how we can create an appropriate space for dialogue.

Samuel Klein compared two dialogue meetings that he had recently attended. One meeting started with everybody introducing themselves. Essentially, each person summarised their CV. Information was exchanged but little genuine dialogue occurred. At the other meeting, participants were asked to get into pairs and look at each other in silence for one minute. Much more was accomplished. Real personal connections were established through this creative approach which recognised how much communication can occur in silence. People were asked to have the courage to look one another in the eye as individual people, rather than looking at their notes and presenting themselves as professionals. If we try to achieve dialogue in an organisational context, we need to constantly consider what kind of communication we are facilitating and to explore different tools for improving the quality of that communication.

Story is a valuable tool. In narrative mediation, an approach to conflict resolution proposed by John Winslade and Gerald Monk, participants are invited to recognise that they have a preconceived story about the other parties, and to tell that story.[6] As the stories are told, the orthodoxies of participants' conceptions of the other are identified and can be challenged. If participants maintain an attitude of respect towards the others for having the courage to turn up, and if a skilled facilitator can create a space in which people feel able to speak, this can be a powerful process. Samuel Klein, discussing the merits of the approach, noted that in dialogue it is valuable to have the stories we tell about each other on the table so that we can see them for what they are, and realise that they are malleable.

---

6   See John Winslade and Gerald Monk, *Narrative Mediation: a New Approach to Conflict Resolution*, (Jossey Bass, 2000), *Practicing Narrative Mediation: Loosening the Grip of Conflict*, (Jossey Bass, 2008).

Of course, different approaches to dialogue may be suited to different contexts. Imam Sajid highlighted the need for well-researched, civil, persistent dialogue with the media to challenge damaging misrepresentations of particular groups. Sarah Perceval made the important observation that getting together to have some fun is as valid a form of dialogue as any.

Sometimes dialogue participants differ in their motivations and in the level of interaction in which they are prepared to engage, just as a young teacher may differ from his pupils on the purpose and priorities of their lessons (Samuel Klein). Fitting the approach to the situation, and negotiating a form of worthwhile dialogue in which all are prepared to participate is part of the creative work dialogue facilitation.

Effectiveness in Dialogue for Conflict Transformation

This article highlights some key insights from our third 'Making Dialogue Effective' panel discussion, with conflict transformation experts Dr Diana Francis and Dr Marwan Darweish. The 'transformation' approach recognises conflict as a potential catalyst for positive change, when it can be dealt with creatively. A comprehensive approach, it seeks to engage and transform attitudes, relationships, discourses, sometimes even social structures, rather than simply managing the destructive effects of conflict. The insights of conflict transformation specialists on dialogue consequently have particular relevance to those working in community dialogue in non-conflict situations, whose primary concerns are attitudes, relationships and discourses.

Previous panel discussions had highlighted the intrinsic value of dialogue, as an inherently transformative, essential human function. Diana Francis noted that while it may be right to recognise dialogue's intrinsic value, facilitators in conflict situations want more from it too; they want it to have a positive outcome in relation to the conflict. Further, dialogue in conflict situations, Marwan Darweish suggested, must be constantly put in the context of this purpose if they are to have an effect on the conditions of injustice which led to conflict. When participants shy away from the difficult issues which divide them, the roots of hostility and violence are left undisturbed.

Prospective dialogue participants and facilitators in situations of conflict face particular challenges. To even begin non-aggressive communication represents a considerable achievement in a situation where two groups generally see each other as the enemy, and blame each other for numerous very painful events. Further, conflict situations typically involve major disparities of power, and the disempowered group may be unwilling to talk peacefully with the other group for fear of normalising an unbearable situation. Marwan Darweish cited a case in which, for this reason, it was not possible to organise a face-to-face Israeli-Palestinian dialogue. However, both parties were willing to work for change in their own communities, and wanted to hear about the efforts of the other group through an independent mediator. This indirect form of dialogue opened a space for a new discourse and further dialogue. Diana Francis noted that often, in a situation of entrenched hostility, there will be 'soft edges', a few people on each side who want to do something. They provide a starting point. In tense conflict situations facilitators have to be creative and seek out the beginnings of dialogue.

Where face-to-face dialogue can be achieved in the context of conflict, there are inevitably difficulties. Emotions run high and may be explosive. It is difficult to avoid a bitter exchange of stories of suffering, and of blame. Then, there is a risk that the achievements of dialogue at one level of society will be undermined because they are unconnected to other levels - something that those working in community dialogue can relate to.

Power relationships from outside the dialogue space may be uncomfortably replicated within it, for instance, through awareness that one group and not the other has been in a position to fund the project. Sometimes external power relationships are reversed; participants from a cultural or ethnic group which has persecuted the group to which the others belong are constantly on the back foot, even if they themselves have opposed that persecution.

To manage such dialogues, facilitators work to achieve a set of conditions in which, despite the various obstacles, a constructive dialogue can take place. Diana Francis listed some key conditions. An assurance of physical safety is essential, as is freedom from time pressure. It is very important to hold the dialogue on neutral ground, where none of the participants will feel that the other immediately has the upper hand. Marwan Darweish referred to an Israeli-Palestinian dialogue which was held in a kibbutz; for the first day discussion was limited to the question of why there was water for irrigation in the kibbutz but no drinking water on the West Bank. Community dialogue organisers need to consider ownership of space too; even in non-conflict situations participants may feel inhibited by feeling that they are guests in another group's space.

Equality of representation is another important condition, which is again worth considering in community dialogue. Participants may feel less at ease if the numbers, or the level of education/experience of the groups, are very uneven. It is also important to have an agreed purpose and clear protocol, so that everyone consents to the process and knows what is expected of them.

Finally, an appropriate facilitator, with permission and intention to 'police' the agreed process, is essential. Marwan Darweish noted that it is sometimes crucial to have an impartial facilitator, who can provide reflections without being seen to speak for one or other party. The facilitator can provide a model of calm, respectful engagement. As Diana Francis noted, he/she has a crucial role to play in providing psychological safety, giving people confidence that they will not be trampled over or ignored and that the proceedings will not be allowed to deteriorate.

Undoubtedly facilitators and organisers of community dialogue can learn from the insights of those who work in conflict situations. Certain details that need to be attended to in order to make a dialogue possible in a conflict situation may not determine the viability of community dialogue in non-conflict situations. However, such details may have a profound effect on the quality of such dialogue.

Skills in Dialogue: Cultivating Listening and Empathy

Part I

Effective, or 'quality' dialogue, as discussed in various 'Making Dialogue Effective' discussions, is an intrinsically valuable expression of our humanity which may also increase mutual understanding, promote friendship or even help us to address conflict. As one of our panellists for this session noted, it provides an important way of thinking through who we are, and who we are in relation to others, providing space to explore the complexity of our identities (Justine Huxley). But what skills do participants and facilitators need to ensure quality dialogue? Dialogue facilitator Lisa Cumming, Justine Huxley of St Ethelburga's Centre for Reconciliation and Peace, and Dr Jill Adam of Level Partnerships joined us to consider the question. Part I of this article on the discussion looks at what is needed for dialogue at the level of individual participants.

Lisa Cumming adjusted the terms of the question, suggesting that what we are looking for in dialogue are not so much 'skills' as qualities. Quality dialogue, perhaps, requires something more integral to the participants' outlook than 'skills'.

What, then, are the most important qualities for dialogue participants to possess? Our panellists highlighted the following qualities: self-awareness, resilience, imagination, a sense of our common humanity, motivation, curiosity and a quality of real presence and attention.

Lisa Cumming referred back to the prerequisites for dialogue suggested by Daniel Yankelovich and discussed by Ute Kelly, identifying the qualities required to secure each of these three conditions.[7] One of the conditions is, in Lisa's terms, that people are okay and open about challenging assumptions. This, she suggested, requires not only a level of self-awareness but also a certain self-confidence or resilience, because it is incredibly hard to challenge and to be challenged.

---

7   See Daniel Yankelovich, *The Magic of Dialogue,* (Simon and Schuster, 1999) and Discussion I in this volume.

Skills in Dialogue: Cultivating Listening and Empathy

Part 2

In part 1 of this article we looked at the skills, or qualities, that enable quality dialogue to happen. Our panellists suggested that such dialogue requires self-awareness, resilience, imagination, a sense of our common humanity, motivation, curiosity and a quality of real presence and attention.

Part 2 of this article will explore how these qualities may be instilled in the general population. First, though, we should consider what skills and qualities the facilitators of dialogue need to play their key role.

Part of their role is to model the attitudes that will enable real dialogue to develop. For example, by themselves developing an attitude of curiosity about the identities and experience of participants they can encourage participants to take a similar positive interest in each other (Justine Huxley).

Facilitators also need the skills to *manage* the process through a series of balancing acts. Facilitators need to balance safety and free expression. Lisa Cummings recalled an example of genuine dialogue occurring when people were shouting at each other; the discussion was very heated but participants were genuinely listening to each other. Facilitators must police the fine line between heated communication and uncontrolled emotional outbursts.

Another key balance to strike is between attention to the technical aspects of dialogue and surrender to the mystery of it (Lisa Cumming). A range of tools and strategies can help promote honest talk but a facilitator should not become enslaved to them. Lisa cited Peter Kellett's description of dialogue as a place where 'deep things get expressed, new possibilities emerge and often the boundaries of self and other melt away.'[9] Dialogue cannot be fully planned and controlled; it is a journey of discovery (Jill Adam).

The tools and techniques of dialogue are diverse. Justine Huxley discussed the use of story and personal narrative, which she has found a precious tool for generating empathy. For example, in an early dialogue at St Ethelburga's between

---

9   Peter M. Kellett, *Conflict Dialogue: Working With Layers of Meaning for Productive Relationships*, (California: Sage Publications, 2007), 58.

people with strongly held opposite views on abortion, personal stories played a very important role in humanising a tense discussion. 'What in your life has brought you to this position?' was a crucial question for the facilitator to ask. A recent St Ethelburga's' resource explores the range of ways in which story can be used in dialogue.[10]

A well-equipped dialogue facilitator may be able to lead dialogue participants into quality dialogue. But who can nurture the qualities for dialogue in potential dialogue participants, that is, in the general population? Given our panellist's insight that dialogue requires not so much skills as more deeply engrained qualities, it is perhaps not surprising that the role of parents was discussed. Empathy, for example, can only be developed when it is experienced, and parents generally provide the crucial early experiences of empathy. Lisa Cumming noted that as a parent she felt entirely responsible for the humanisation of her child. Where parents are, for whatever reason, ill-equipped for this role, other relatives and friends, charity initiatives or professional agencies may be able to compensate to some degree for this severe disadvantage.

Professional educators also have a role to play in instilling the qualities we have identified as important for dialogue. Lisa Cumming cited Bhikhu Parekh's vision of education as humanisation, not just socialisation. Education, he holds, should 'develop the power of independent thought, analysis and criticism,' and 'cultivate... a sympathetic imagination.'[11] The role of schools should not be confined to the teaching of skills. Apart from specific activities designed to introduce children to intercultural dialogue, the ethos of schools and the example and encouragement of teachers can help foster the qualities that dialogue requires. In diverse contexts teachers take up the great challenges of humanising and of teaching sensitively about diverse cultures and religions. The nature of the challenge varies; the issues faced by a teacher in a rural, uniformly white and middleclass school will differ from those faced by a teacher in a diverse inner-city school (Jill Adam). Some teachers face the additional challenge of catering for children living with poverty or even abuse.

Universities may also contribute to the development of qualities for dialogue at a crucial point in the development of young adults. There are some interesting examples of creative initiatives. For instance, a university in New Zealand adopted

---

10 'What's your story?' St Ethelburga's Centre for Reconciliation and Peace, accessed 22nd May 2012, http://stethelburgas.org/narrative-resource

11 See Bhikhu Parekh, *Rethinking Multiculturalism: Cultural Diversity and Political Theory*, (Houndmills Basingstoke; London: Macmillan Press ltd, 2000), 227.

the idea of Maori meeting houses[12] in which groups come together and work things out.

One of the concrete measures towards greater dialogue literacy that was identified was the practice of recognising and resourcing good practice in all kinds of dialogue initiatives (Lisa Cumming). The regrettable truth is that the current economic climate limits resources for such projects. The best community, as Jill Adam noted, is very expensive. However, much can be achieved through volunteering, gifts of time and resources, and by people simply taking time to be human, to communicate and share ideas. Fittingly, another concrete measure proposed by Lisa Cumming was for a few people really passionate about dialogue to get together and reflect further on possible actions. People who believe in the creative power of dialogue should naturally look to that very process to find ways of promoting the skills and qualities upon which quality dialogue depends.

---

12 Among the Maori, the indigenous people of New Zealand, each sub-tribe or *hapu* has a gathering place called a *marae*, with a communal meeting house called a *wharenui*. The *wharenui* is the site of semi-structured discussions, debates and presentations, as well as being used for certain funeral rites and doubling as a sleeping house (*wharemoe*) for guests. See Spencer Lilley, 'The Marae as an information ground,' http://ibec.ischool. washington.edu/maraeig.php

Discussion 5

Becoming a Dialogue Movement: What Can Dialogue Learn from Other Movements?

Local intercultural dialogue efforts may have a real impact on the quality of the relationships of those involved. But how can dialogue have a larger-scale, more pervasive effect on our society? In a 2010 Dialogue Society discussion, Revd Donald Reeves suggested that dialogue needs to become a movement. Dr Nicola Montagna of Middlesex University, and environmental author and activist Danny Chivers joined Dialogue Society Executive Director Ozcan Keles to discuss what the 'Dialogue Movement' can learn from other movements.

Nicola Montagna explained that academics typically define a 'social movement' as 'a specific form of collective mobilisation which engages conflict by means of unconventional forms of protest.' It is an unorthodox form of political participation, with protest as the main form of action. Social movements are horizontally organised, relying on informal networks rather than hierarchies. They are engaged in some form of conflict and propose alternatives to existing systems. Scholars often differentiate proactive movements such as the Civil Rights Movement or the Environmental Movement, which promote social and political change, and reactive movements, such as the Anti-Immigration Movement and the No-Tax Movement, which resist social change.

This dominant definition excludes any 'Dialogue Movement'. While people engaged in dialogue generally aspire to social change, the change envisaged is a more harmonious relationship between different groups; protest and engagement in conflict would not serve this vision. Social movements focus on particular issues, exposing a perceived present or imminent wrong and calling for action to redress or prevent it. Dialogue is not issue-focused but relationship-focused; it is about bringing people together *regardless* of their differences on various issues. While dialogue involves building up forums where crucial issues can be discussed, and while some people involved are motivated by its capacity to do so, it is not tied to a particular issue. For a social movement as defined above, cultivating good relationships with people with different views

21. Try to make your venue a warm, comfortable and pleasant environment. Ensure, as a bare minimum, that it is clean, tidy and at a comfortable temperature.

22. Promote a sense of equality in the dialogue by holding it in a neutral location.

23. Pay attention to equality of representation; if one group in a dialogue is considerably smaller, or at a clear disadvantage in terms of education or experience, they may feel uncomfortable.

24. Try to achieve a balance in terms of gender, culture, religion, age, social group etc.

25. Use simple 'ice-breaker' games and activities to help participants feel at ease and to warm people up, encouraging participation.

26. It will often be helpful to begin a dialogue session by introducing and seeking agreement on some basic ground rules. You may want to offer some advice on listening skills and helpful attitudes for dialogue (see 'Participating in Dialogue' section below).

27. Be aware that it can often be counterproductive to put pressure on the process of dialogue by being too prescriptive and rigid about what it should achieve. Dialogue is an unpredictable process of human interaction and tends to benefit from space to develop organically.

28. This does not mean that you do not need any sense of purpose, only that it is frequently beneficial to keep the aim broad or flexible. The planning and management of your event will need to be guided by some kind of goal, even if it is as broad and open as 'maximise opportunities for natural, relaxed dialogue'. In certain contexts, and to appeal to certain participants, more specific aims may need to be stated.

29. In situations of conflict there will need to be particular clarity about the purpose and process of the gathering; people will need to know exactly what to expect before engaging.

30. Ensure physical safety.

31. Minimise time pressure.

32. Food can be a good ice-breaker, get people talking and encourage natural human interaction.

33. Where possible, intersperse formal dialogue sessions with other activities. A lot of valuable interaction can happen during recreational trips or activities, over food, or even on the bus between venues.

Techniques/approaches to try

34. Remember that silence can be an effective vehicle for dialogue.

35. Use personal narrative (asking people to tell their own stories) as a way of generating empathy.

36. Challenge preconceptions by inviting participants to tell the stories that they have about others ('narrative mediation' – John Winslade and Gerald Monk[15]).

37. A 'talking object' can be a helpful tool to ensure that everybody has the chance to speak without being interrupted. Only the person holding the object (for example, a stone or teddy) is allowed to speak. The object can be passed around a circle of people.

38. Remember the value of people coming together just to have some fun (for example, telling entertaining stories or having a party).

39. Work with what you have. In conflict situations, where any form of dialogue is profoundly challenging, facilitators have to take advantage of any willingness to engage. Low-level, indirect communication through a facilitator is a start worth making where face-to face engagement is not possible.

40. In intrafaith dialogue, engaging at the level of scripture can be helpful; even a 'hardline' group hostile to dialogue may engage when you appeal to a source whose authority they accept.

Tips for good facilitation

41. Accept people's inevitably varied motives for coming to a dialogue event, and work with them.

42. As a facilitator, model the behaviour and attitudes you hope to see in the group (for instance, calm, respectful engagement and curiosity about others.)

43. Encourage engagement at a personal, informal level.

44. Be aware of the sensitivities of participants and navigate these gently and tactfully.

45. Gently try to draw the more reticent participants into the conversation.

46. Do not put too much pressure on people to participate in ways that they are not comfortable with. Some people may want to attend, listen and learn the first time they attend, without speaking. They may have the confidence to speak next time.

47. Balance safety and freedom of expression; destructive emotional outbursts need to be controlled, but sometimes genuine dialogue can happen in loud voices and heated exchanges.

---

15 See John Winslade and Gerald Monk, *Narrative Mediation: a New Approach to Conflict Resolution,* (Jossey Bass, 2000), *Practicing Narrative Mediation: Loosening the Grip of Conflict,* (Jossey Bass, 2008).

70. If somebody addresses you in a negative or disrespectful way, try not to respond in the same manner. Try to use it as an opportunity to explain your perspective further or more clearly, turning the situation into something positive.

71. Be ready to challenge assumptions, others' and your own. This is difficult and requires resilience.

72. Listen to others with empathy, using imagination to try to understand their perspectives and feelings. Step outside the bubble of your own concerns and try to see others as people in their own right.

73. When attending organised dialogue, try to do a little research about the topic of dialogue and the group. This will give you background knowledge and perhaps more confidence and more to contribute.

74. Be aware of the messages you send by body language and clothing even before you speak. Ensure that your body language does not send out negative signals or contradict what you are saying.

75. Remember that dialogue is not debate or discussion. It is not about winning an argument or proving a point, and it need not end in consensus. Participants should not try to persuade or convert. Dialogue is about listening to one another and growing in mutual understanding.

76. Make a conscious effort to be fully present, avoiding distractions.

77. Try to focus on what the other person can teach you, rather than on how you are going to respond.

78. Respect other participants; if nothing else, they have had the courage to engage.

79. Do not force your viewpoint on others and try not to get defensive. Respect the fact that others will have different perspectives and views and be ready to agree to disagree.

80. Be respectful and considerate. Think about the impact of *how* you say something. Be aware of the context and the connotations that certain words or phrases may have. Try to avoid putting things in ways that will cause offence or hurt. Being truthful does not require being brutal.

81. The way you behave and how you treat others may say more than your actual words. Try to have a positive effect on the quality of the dialogue by setting an example of respectful engagement and listening.

Recommended Reading

Bohm, David. *On Dialogue*. London: Routledge, 2004.

Bohm, David, Donald Factor and Peter Garrett. *Dialogue- A Proposal,* 1991. http://www.david-bohm.net/dialogue/dialogue_proposal.html

Buber, Martin. *I and Thou*. New York: Simon and Schuster, 1971.

Buber, Martin. *Between Man and Man*. London, Routledge, 2002.

Dialogue Society. *Community Dialogue Manual* series. London: Dialogue Society, 2012. http://www.dialoguesociety.org/publications/community.html

Isaacs, William. *Dialogue and the Art of Thinking Together*. New York: Bantam Doubleday Dell, 1999.

Kellett, Peter M. *Conflict Dialogue: Working With Layers of Meaning for Productive Relationships*. Thousand Oaks, California: Sage Publications, 2007.

Kelly, Ute and Lisa Cumming. *Civil Society Supporting Dialogue and Deliberation*. Carnegie UK Trust, 2010.

Kurucan, Ahmet and Mustafa Kasim Erol. *Dialogue in Islam*. London: Dialogue Society, 2012. http://www.dialoguesociety.org/publications/community/720-dialogue-in-islam.html

Murithi, Timothy. 'Practical Peacemaking Wisdom from Africa: Reflections on Ubuntu.' *The Journal of Pan African Studies* 1:4 (June 2006).

Parekh, Bhikhu. *Rethinking Multiculturalism: Cultural Diversity and Political Theory*. Houndmills, Basingstoke; London: Macmillan Press ltd, 2000.

Sener, Omer and Frances Sleap. *Dialogue Theories*. Edited by Paul Weller. London: Dialogue Society, 2013.

St Ethelburga's Centre for Reconciliation and Peace. 'What's your story?' Accessed 22nd May 2012. http://stethelburgas.org/narrative-resource

Talk for a Change. *We need to talk about.....Can discussing controversial issues strengthen community relations?* Talk for a Change, 2012. http://www.talkforachange.co.uk/wp-content/themes/haworth/publications/We%20Need%20To%20Talk%20About.pdf

Winslade, John and Gerald Monk. *Narrative Mediation: a New Approach to Conflict Resolution*. San Francisco, CA: Jossey Bass, 2000.

Winslade, John and Gerald Monk. *Practicing Narrative Mediation: Loosening the Grip of Conflict*. San Francisco, CA: Jossey Bass, 2008.

Yankelovich, Daniel. *The Magic of Dialogue*. New York: Simon and Schuster,

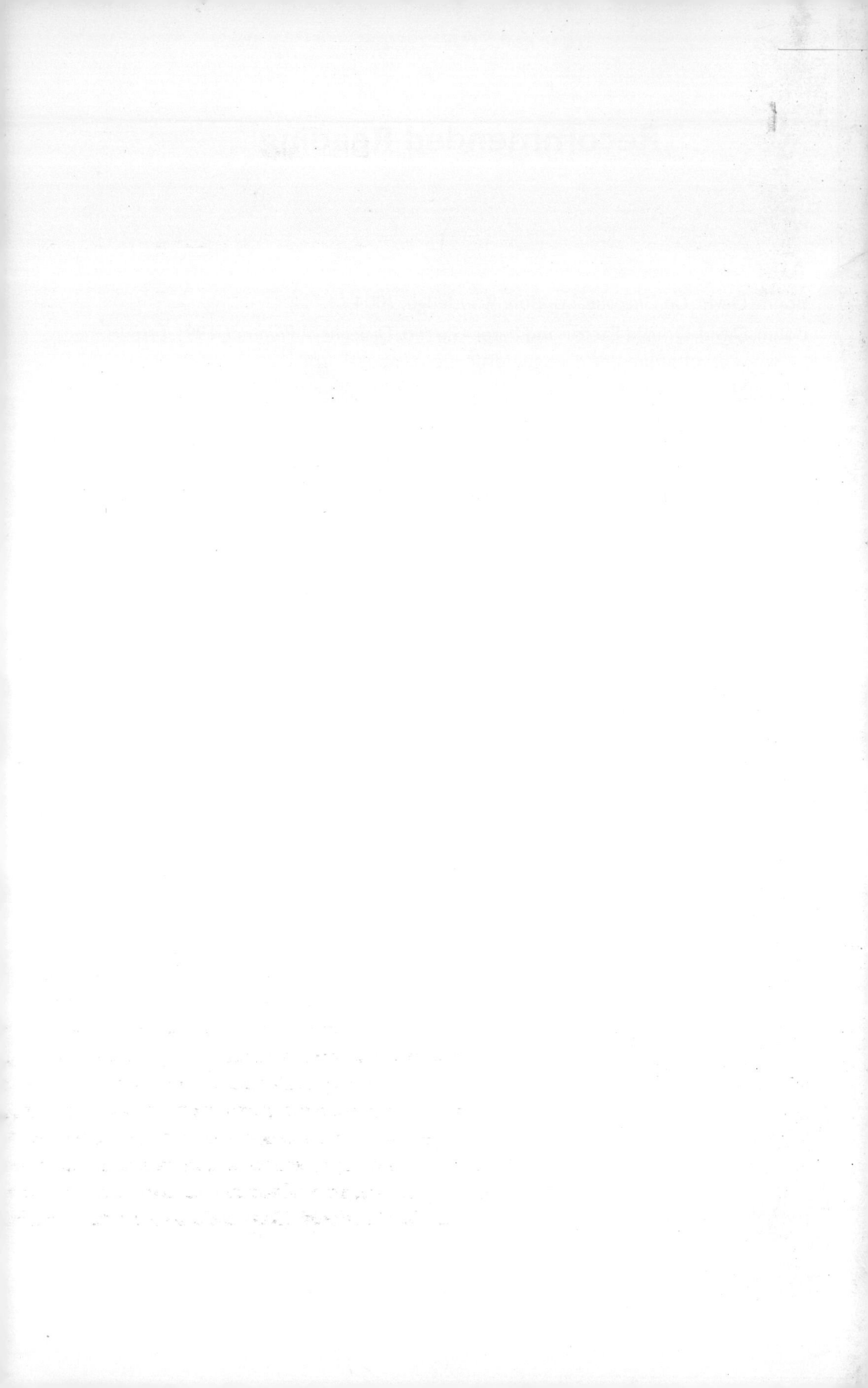